INSOMNIA IN ANOTHER TOWN

Lisa M. Hase-Jackson

CLEMSON
LITERATURE SERIES
CONVERSE

As a partnership between Clemson University Press and the Converse College Low-Residency MFA program, this series publishes poetry collections, short-story collections, and creative nonfiction.

Titles in the series
Ice on a Hot Stove, edited by Denise Duhamel and Rick Mulkey
89% by Sarah Cooper
crossing over by Kim Shegog

INSOMNIA IN ANOTHER TOWN

Lisa M. Hase-Jackson

CLEMSON
UNIVERSITY
PRESS

Cover design by Lindsay Scott
Cover image by Linda Briskin
Typeset in Minion Pro by Gloria J. Aragon

For information about Clemson University Press,
please visit our website at www.clemson.edu/press.

CONTENTS

III

One Saturday in March

Gary researches chicken psychology
after finding a patch of gold feathers
scattered in the backyard

and we realize that Buttercup is gone.
He wants to know if the other
three hens will miss her, if they are

traumatized by her attack
and sudden disappearance.
The barred owl that had been

visiting the bird bath for the last
week, conspicuously quiet,
apparently gaining from our loss.

Living on the farm, I used to fish
the creek bordering my land, slipping
sinkers on the line to keep

it taut and tense, which is how I feel now.
One little chicken shouldn't cause
this much sorrow, Gary

says, but there is no small grief,
I say. All are interconnected;
one touch sends tremors

through our core
like the fly in the web
that wakes the spider at its center.

It's been 20 years since I left the farm
and I still remember every chicken
lost to a coyote

or feral dog. Gary rakes
Buttercup's feathers and places
them in an empty feed bag

that he deposits in the trash
bin. The three surviving
hens graze greening grass

around us, sticking close
to the shed, the shadow
of the house. Goldie

is the only brown chicken
now. The other two
open ranks to let her in.

I

SHE FLIES WITH HER OWN WINGS

When the band loaded up
for the road trip from Kansas City
to Tacoma there wasn't enough space
for the sewing machine my mother
wanted to bring—to have something
to do while my father's band
practiced long into the night. She had a keen eye
for fashion—always understood color
and lines like no one else I ever knew.

Maybe it didn't matter since the band dissolved
as soon they reached Tacoma, before even
the first night of their gig, and there my parents were,
Dad jobless, my mother pregnant. Portland
was less expensive, so that's where they moved—
where they brought into the world their first
and only child whom they tucked into the top drawer
of a dresser in their partially furnished apartment.
Dad finally found a job working

in a record store somewhere not in Portland;
sometimes it is Haight Asbury, sometimes near L.A.
I've heard it both ways.
Mom found work too, demonstrating
how to use weight-loss machines
at a women's gym nearby
leaving me with a neighbor,
only to be fired a couple of days later
when the manager figured out
Mom had recently given birth, that's how thin
she was. Not knowing

how to reach Dad, she called
her mother, Mary, who wired money
for a bus ticket back home. My father
joined us a few weeks later.

"Umbrella Man"

Your grandpa is named for a poet,
          my mother tells me,
and rumored
          to have
robbed banks,
          to have
been a boxer,
          to have
burned the courthouse down.

          toodle-uma-lama-toodle-ay,
          toodle-uma-lama-toodle-ay,

she sings,
          tying my saddle shoes in Grandma's kitchen.

          Any umb-a-rellas, any umb-a-rellas
          to mend today?

Grandpa smokes hand-rolled cigarettes at the kitchen table—
          drum tobacco—a constellation of ember-burned craters
pitting yellow linoleum beneath his chair.

          Grandpa doesn't hear

          toodle-uma-lama-toodle-ay,
          toodle-uma-lama-toodle-ay,

He keeps his hearing aid turned low.

Years of nights and overtime at the printing press
          for a two-bedroom house and six
                    noisy, in-and-out-all-the-time runaway kids.

          Bring your parasol, it may be small, it may be big,

Powel Byron Thomas; P.B. for short.
          Everyone calls him Tommy.

          He repairs them all with what you call a thingamajig.

Rummaging in his steel tool box of oiled tools, worn and thrown,
    notions-filled baby food jars.

        Grandpa repairs outdoor furniture,

their spines and canvas skins

    He'll mend your umbrella, then go on his way,

with nine fingers and only one thumb.

        singing toodle-uma-lama-toodle-ay,
        toodle-uma-lama-toodle-ay,
        any umbrellas to fix today?

Most common injury among press operators.

Nocturne I

Musician's nights
        ebb easily into early morning
and people often drift
        to our house after the final set
for a last drink,
        another hour of song.
Smoky timbre of voices
        hang in the warmth of my room
as I will my father
        to tuck me in
as my mother promised.

His light brown hair,
        rock-star long and weightless
as gossamer, brushes my eyelids
        as he kisses my forehead.
Look, he says, turning his ear
        toward me.
Can you wiggle your ears like this?
        I am wrapped in blankets,
so it must be winter. Laughter
        and light rising from the living room
infuse his hair.
        When I show him that I can
he whisks me around the living room
        to show the other adults,
giggles spilling all over their laps
        because my father didn't know
I'd wiggle my ears like that,
        as easy as blinking an eye,
or breathing.

Nocturne II

Even placed in proper context,
memories conflate—like ivy
planted yards apart, they find
each other, intertwine again—
braided ropes of mystery and dream.

Always there are late nights, music
in every nook. My father returns home
early, guitar neck broken.
He and other men from the band,
        one who plays drums,
        and one who plays trumpet,
look over the dreadnought,
unplugged and glinting red
beneath the heavy lamp
swinging above the kitchen table,
        the only illumination in the house.

This broken-necked gittern
is our livelihood, what keeps
nights lively, lights on,
food in the fridge.

Questions of
        How will it be fixed?
saturate pre-dawn amber, tugging at cigarette
smoke and the aroma of stale wine,
        heavy as the house.

Nocturne III

My father finds steady work
helping the trumpet player
manage a nightclub at the Gatehouse
apartments. His day starts when the sun's
intentions toward the western prairie
are plain, and when the scales he practices
rise above the steam of his shower.
I sing along from the hall.

My mother divides her thick hair
into pigtails, lays each over a shoulder.
Yellow is her favorite color. She cups
my cheeks with patchouli scented palms,
checks my face for crumbs. Her fingers
feather-soft and cool.

Before day's final disintegration,
red votive candles are lit and placed
upon round tables around the club.
The drink my mother orders
from the man behind the bar surrounded
by stools arrives in a stemmed glass, contains
an olive. My father has gone to sit on the top step
of the sunken-floor nook in the next room,
guitar on his knee, fingers finding strings
until their path is deliberate, their purpose
finding cadence as he picks the cord for *Moon Shadow*
or *House of the Rising Sun.*
People gather to listen to him play,
watch as he slips away, like an illusion,
into song.

BRIDGE

Headlights in the rearview mirror
mask my mother's delicate face
in white as she steers the car's
giant wheel with hands meant
for art. Her mouth is set
in an *I've made this decision*
sort of way I am just coming
to understand. My father is not
in the car with us; he sits in the apartment
back in Topeka. When the signal is clear,
Sweet City Woman and *Bobby McGee*
come through on the radio. Otherwise,
static. Mom digs around in her hobo bag
to find enough change on the bottom
to pay the toll due at the other end
of the turnpike pouring into Kansas City.
There is no small talk. She drives
through rivulets of familiar streets
to her mother's house who is somehow
expecting us.

WASHINGTON STREET

I'd thrown a handful of rocks at a car
passing by my grandmother's house
on the suggestion of Walter
who lived down the street. I wasn't sorry.

Only surprised the car had stopped,
that the person inside was a person at all,
then angry she'd marched to the door
of my grandmother's house, told. I frowned

at that car and its driver, the boy who slipped away,
my own failure to hide in the ditch
and my parents' divorce the month before.
How brief the catharsis, pebbles pinging

against metal and glass, power and anger
jettisoning gravel and sand.

WINTER, INDEPENDENCE

In the basement apartment one morning, I wake to snow. The backyard is a perfect square of white. No grass, no twigs, trees laden and still; sky a sheet of unlined paper. Beyond the glass door, dry fluff and quiet. Snow is still new to me, unspoiled by years of shoveling, of snowballs to the face.

Mike Ballou comes to visit in his tall hat and cowboy boots. He is tall, too. I like Mike Ballou. He pays attention to me, sometimes. Mike's footprints lead from the side gate to the sliding glass doors. The snow is not perfect anymore.

I walk in circles and spirals, then crossways like a checkerboard, imagine the intricate trails I leave behind, something like the footprints in comics, as perfect as the soles of my shoes, a wordless story of my day.

LATCHKEY

a navigation of city blocks
trees   presidents   drives
parameters and boundaries
never to cross alone
the thick smell of summer
asphalt   bare feet
the gaseous glow
of streetlamps   Home
is an   empty refrigerator,
a tin filled with dimes
    luxurious fare for the city bus

                        on the prairie woods stand
                        and though I can't feel it from where
                        I stand I know wind strums the legs of cottonwood
                                rushes deciduous leaves into
                        creeks filled with crawdads
                        and silt   Flint

news-papered windows set deep in adobe walls
        a hollow living room we are hidden
mornings a hostile school bus
indifferent eyes   sour laughter
unfinished homework   Weekends
untethered   and goat-head stickers in
calloused heels   a shortcut through Roosevelt park
        a hill too steep
a speeding skateboard   the gravel
   the slide
                    the scrape
                            the burn

HER OWN GIRL

When Mom answered
the woman who asked
      whose little girl I was
that I was my own person,
      that I did not *belong* to anyone,

there was a pause,
one might call it pregnant,
because no one expected
her to answer that way.

I stood quiet, too,
because I wanted
her to claim me
      to say that I belonged
to her and she to me,
      that we belonged
together like no other two people
in the world.

That was our first year
in Albuquerque,
her first semester
      at the college; the year
of Darwinism and feminism,
      of never telling
      your child no,

the summer of painting
      back to bananas and trees
on our neighbor, Quintin's,
VW bug,
      and the year he drove
his motorcycle off the side
of a mountain.

When I walked away
      unannounced from camp
that summer, found the restaurant
where she worked
using landmarks and pointed questions,

she made an extra house key
I tied around my neck with yarn,
        then she showed me how
to take the city bus
        to the grocery store
and the laundry mat—
        how to use the bus map.

In late August
we walked together to
        Eugene Field
Elementary,

to UNM campus,
        where we found a structure
near the art department
we called the rook
because of its resemblance
to the chess piece,
        our meeting place
for the next four years.

There were a dozen other little tricks
she showed me, too,
        tricks to help me become
my own little girl.

Coal Street Magi

First Christmas in Albuquerque.
There's enough money for food
and bus fare, but not for things a Pell Grant
doesn't consider. It never occurred
to me there was never *really* a plan,
then, or when we had arrived in July.
It was always *let's see what happens.*

On the 24th, Mom brought home a tumbleweed
she'd found trapped against a chain link fence
as if it was the most natural thing in the world
to spray-paint it white with leftover paint
found in the art room rubbage
and stick it, stem down, into a Folger's coffee can
filled with sand from the alley beside our apartment.

We strung popcorn and cranberries on needle and thread,
taped construction-paper garland we draped around
the bush's brittle frame; fashioned an aluminum-foil star
for the top. If we'd a camera, we'd have taken photos,
I'm sure, though the flash might have set
the whole thing ablaze. Dinner was peanut butter
and jam on saltine crackers until my stomach swelled
(I've never eaten them again). We stayed up late,
read and listened for bells in the desert, fell asleep
in our clothes. Morning we found on our stoop
a used toaster, bag of fruit, a copy of *Big Bird's Busy Book.*
No card, no note, and none of our neighbors,
not Quinten, Jim, nor Linda & Diane,
ever took credit.

AFTER THE BAN

Barbie was never allowed
into the one-room studio apartments
of my early childhood. *Epitome
of sexism* my mother said.
A bad influence.

I played with Fisher Price people
and fire trucks instead,
hosting water-for-tea parties with plush animals
quietly while Mom studied.

Out of the blue (and into the pink),
my mother lifted the ban on Barbie
because her early-childhood professor said
excluding Barbie from a child's repertoire
denied her hours of imaginative play
(though I wonder what that professor would say
to the prevalence of body dysmorphia
among girls who play with Barbie today).

The price of a real Barbie, Lexus
among fashion dolls, was more
than I could spend. Only knock-offs
from the TG&Y, coarse hair
springing from heads that popped
easily off and faces prone to concave,
found their way to my toy chest

until Christmas when I unwrapped
a real Barbie, the scent of fresh
soft plastic clinging to my pajamas,
my hair. Our bohemian lifestyle
of tie dye and paisley, of art studios
and second-run movies, incense
and crystals seemed shabbier, more tattered
           around the edges that day.
Being broke felt more like being poor

and I noticed more keenly the absence
of money and clothes, of certain types of food
in the fridge. Rather than becoming whatever
I wanted, as my mother encouraged,
I wanted all that was Barbie instead.

"Meep and Mope"

Mom wrote a book one time,
titled *Meep and Mope,*
about two pretend characters
not unlike the two of us.
They lived together alone

far from familiar streets,
walked or took the bus
most everywhere, hitchhiking
when it came to leaving town.

She used her budding drawing skills,
filled their world with watercolors,
finished the story with her own quirk

then sent the book to a publisher
with seldom hope. Like the narcissist
professor who criticized her work
the semester before, the editors
rejected it straight away;
both our feelings were hurt.
I had no chance to reread

or claim it before she threw the book away;
hadn't known until I asked one day
about the future adventures of Meep and Mope
when they resumed their story in books two, three,
and four. Mom just shrugged and turned back
to her text leaving me to grieve newly lost
found friends, for that is how I saw
those pretend characters
based on her and me.

What Brought You Here

after Dorianne Laux

Repent nothing. Not the late nights
reading trashy romance novels
or the hours watching late night television.
Not the unsavory phone conversations
with randy boys who found your number
printed under "teenager's phone"
in the white pages. Not
the homework left crumpled
at the bottom of a putty-gray locker.
Don't regret those. Not the nights
you cursed your father's name—
or your stepmother's— laid out on the bed
of your lonely unkempt room. Don't regret
the unkempt room. You were meant
to smoke stolen cigarettes at your bedroom
window, crush aluminum cans in the basement
to cash in. You were meant to wear grease-laden
polyester aprons of fast-foodom,
pockets boasting shriveled
fries, a wilted bit of lettuce. You tried to organize
that life and wound up here. Regret none
of it, not one of those frittered, frivolous days
when you knew nothing, when songs
on the radio were the only prayers
you believed in, loving them for their
refrains, their unspent truth.

Per Aspera

Incessant winds corral women, isolate them for days innumerable and nights undistinguishable. No other but walls for conversation, the wind's constant howl call and response across the plains. No gristled body to shove, no cochlea to receive protest, no slender eyes to bear witness. *No escaping* the wind, like no escaping water on the sea. Snapping limbs, whipping power lines, twisting trees and clapboard siding, glass rain. Branches thrust through shingles … then deluge; tangled stringed locks, robbed breath, skin pummeled with stones, with pebbles, with hail; wind lifting, spinning, dogs and trucks, an entire house. To wait is to bundle under blankets, sit in the dank root cellar with oil lamp and Steinbeck, wool-skein and straight needles, goods canned last year. Sing softly, stifle loudly, it doesn't stop; and never predict. Surrender until zephyr's hum becomes the third voice in your head, the driver of dreams, until trees cease tumult and grasses stand upright, until birds return to the barn loft, to the bath, until finally the world is silent.

"I Dig Rocking Around with You"

—Tom Petty and the Heartbreakers

Abandoned all those
years, the house held an odor
like mold, like mildew.

Something else, too. Wood
shavings, stale alcohol, rank
sweat? We bought the shell,

groomed its hide, rebuilt
raw bones and dressed them in
drywall; sanded wood floors

down to an old blood
stain proving a murder
neighbors told took place in

the dining room: a
man had stomped his wife, like a
bug, to death. Poor, we

couldn't mind. Moved our
couch and stereo beneath
bare studs, open roof,

plugged a floor lamp and
heater into a long cord
connected to the

construction pole left
behind by the construction
crew. We played pool on

weekends, took long drives
along country roads hemmed in
by barbed wire and straw,

watched for deer to poach,
listened to Petty & the
Heartbreakers on tapes

stretched viscous thin, our
car windows rolled down to blow
away smoke, invite

the sweet pungent scent
of alfalfa, skunk musk, road
kill. It was not so

long ago, I can
count the years on toes, on
fingers. Not eons

nor centuries. Nothing like
an eternity.

Planting Season

Harney soil sustains
early green beans
sweet peas,
tomatoes, too; conceals
seed potatoes, carrot seeds,
radishes and grubs.

Black and warm
from the sun's May
rays, loam
collects under nails,
traces the palm's life line.

Will it nourish
this over-ample
garden, and the children,
too? Can it fill
the gaps between
dreams and addiction,
or call me back
to root as I roam
and wander afield?

PRESERVATION

Drive the tractor as your husband
guides the plow. His stubbornness
will require alcohol well before noon.

The day must be dry, the earth warm
the stakes high, made of straight twigs
flagged with strips of cloth, old flannel

will do. Furrow straight as can be managed,
no matter the barrage, and as true as good seed
scattered on warm soil. Remember to stagger

plantings, water well from the house spigot, pray
for rain and a straight back. Pray the neighbors
don't spray herbicide on the pasture across the road

on a day when the wind is from the east and that wildlife
and livestock won't pilfer, that there are no more frosted
mornings.

If luck becomes blooms becomes beans, pick
on a dry day in August and place on ice until ready
for the canner.

Sort Mason jars and Kerr jars, often used for moonshine,
boil to sterilize. Blanch the beans, blanch the lids, pack the jars
and place them under pressure

on the kitchen stove after shooing away the children
but before your husband returns from work,
demanding dinner, quiet, and a can of beer.

Way Out

The 1976 Ford LTD is a shade of yellow
that lands somewhere between Kansas sunflowers

and fog-obscured sun. Today it runs. Its tires
are sound with proper pressure. I buckle the children

into car seats in the back. There is nothing
so concrete against the grim determination

with which everything must be done.
I know the roads, though.

Their dips and washer board patches.
Where the gravel is loose,

where the ditches are steep. I try not to focus
on the magnetism of oncoming traffic.

Semi-trucks hauling trailers the most seductive
but for the children.

Bouts Rimé

Inspired by Edna St. Vincent Millay

Not the first time, nor the last, I lied
to avoid certain future pain,
a state about as unavoidable as rain
or the rising tide.

It's more about what's inside,
like choosing a lane,
that is, whether to leave or to remain.
In the end, I couldn't abide

the constant perpetuation of fear
filling every hour to the brim.
I packed my loyalty, left that place,
grim determination on my face

many years before arriving here.
Still, it wasn't easy. Leaving him.

Land of the Southwind

after Melanie McCabe

I conjure Fox. Kickapoo. Shawnee.
Also, Atchison. Topeka. Burnett. Entreat
the gritty Kaw. Tall figures from history:
John Brown. Carry Nation. Gordon Parks.
Adolescence accompanied by *Dust
in the Wind. Carry on My Wayward Son.*
My cot-caught merger rising above wheat, sorghum,
milo, a rural adoption in tornadic decibels.

I aspire tumultuous atmospheres, green sky before
the hail, combines in the field, morels beneath fallen
elms. In the Chevy's bed, I stack square bales, split
wood, too. Shuffle around slurred speech that seeks
argument, past the pfst of a tab-top can. That man
who used to call me Mouse.

I summon milkweed. Crabapple. Columbine whispers
romance and foolishness. Victory. America's bread
basket. Dorothy's birthplace an impetus for escape.
Passage to Oregon, to Santa Fe, westward expansion
from my mother's Kansas City. Settlers dispersing like birds:
Starlings. Hawks. The incomparable Western Meadowlark.

II

EARLY RELEASE

Beyond the window's grime of top soil
and Wichita smog, vast fields of winter wheat
and milo stubble blocked like a quilt
spread across the western plains,
a ribbon of road unraveling behind
the Goodyear's of a Greyhound
bound for Topeka. His thoughts
flit among dimensional clouds
no longer flattened by twenty-four
months of ramen and Norse
mythology, solitary time
and kitchen duty. No one waiting
just beyond the fence opening
a car door, welcoming him
out like graduation day. How
extraordinarily ordinary
to sit on this bus, the clothes
they took the day he went in
fitting loose as the hide of a malnourished
calf, fifty dollars and a bus ticket stub
back to the county of arrest in his pockets.
Sandalwood scented soap and Old Spice
on his skin, fresh as Christmas
four days away.

RESIDENTIAL MOBILITY

It's hard to learn when moved from one place to the next:
different cities, new neighborhoods, another studio apartment—
changing schools with each. Six times
one year. This school teaches sentence diagramming,
which your mother calls arbitrary, the next
does not. This school embraces new math, this one
the old. This teacher takes an interest in you while another
notices nothing you do. Then there's the teacher
who holds you after school for no reason,
a large woman, who stood on toes you left
sticking out from under your desk after she warned you
not to. You try to fill the gaps in your learning but lose interest
by High School, take the GED, a few community college
satellite courses as a hopeful bridge. Still, you notice a certain look
when you say something not quite right, or even completely
wrong—something everyone learned in third grade but you missed.
Brows wriggling like caterpillars, mouth corners falling like anvils.
You try to work out how you misspoke, backtrack, restate,
wish you had consulted the Internet before you tried to sound
smart, commit deeper to never revealing yourself, to remaining quiet
in mixed company, study more, learn more, go back in time,
restructure your entire life—including choosing different parents,
different passions. You know the bridge in London is not called
the London Bridge, but like running into a pole while riding your bike
because you can't make yourself look elsewhere,
London Bridge is the name that falls out.

SQUALL

Two figures on the bridge in heavy snowfall, charcoal smudges on white canvas. The snow falls fast and heavy on the bridge and on the tin roof of the old red mill, it falls on the creek and on the hills and the black umbrella held by one of the figures standing on the bridge. They are looking out over the water, the two figures, and pointing downstream to something near me. The black umbrella becomes white very quickly and the black lampposts, too, become white, thin like graphite lead from a mechanical pencil, then thread. The two figures stand and stand, diminishing smudges on white canvas. They are engaged in a great conversation about how white the landscape has become in such a short period of time, minutes really. They note how the snow on the tin roof of the old red mill has become thick as a down duvet, how no one has seen the goose that usually swims down river near the old red mill covered in snow that is falling just now.

MAPLE

Spiles tap rising sap
before winter's lapse as spring's
light teases leaves

to unfurl newly
green, bright as the sun and glare.
How resilient

the maple that offers
rising life, liquid and sweet,
without perceived com-

plaint; how fortunate
the man who taps.

Terminal

Lance and Rebecca sit at a table for two in the airport café. They sit and sit. For two weeks, they sit at the table for two in the airport café and are served crepes and imported beer. Their hair is perfect like Ken's and like Barbie's and so is Rebecca's makeup like Barbie's, perfect like a model's; permanent. Travelers who pass Lance and Rebecca sitting at the table for two never remark. They do not know the couples' untold drama. Above the concourse, a hazel ceiling traps mistaken sparrows. They perch above departures and arrivals. Lance and Rebecca have never once noticed the sparrows. They are there still.

Portraiture

On a hot tarmac in Egypt
          or Sudan
a plane is waiting. Beneath my mother's
arm, a wooden case, the one with brass
closures that she carries everywhere, holds
her drawing pencils, paint brushes, a set of watercolors.
She has become who she wanted, like aunt Ruth
who wrote and drew. Mom carries
her slight stature with distracted purpose:
part sprite, part zephyr, skin like olives,
eyes blue flames. She must board soon,
before the stairs are rolled away, but
the wooden box with brass latches sprung
falls like dashed hopes onto the tarmac, pencils
and paintbrushes, cakes of dry hues splayed
and scattered like so much debris.

Dead Birds of the Great Leap Forward

Data linking sparrows to bluebird decline is sparse,
yet sparrows are often blamed for bluebird demise.
An introduced species regarded as invasive,
it's long been acceptable to kill sparrows for no reason at all.

Sparrows are often blamed for bluebird demise,
though bluebirds were not a concern of Mao's.
He viewed sparrows as one of four great pests,
so commanded citizens to bang pots, drive them to the sky.

Bluebird populations were not a concern of Mao's.
He only wished to illustrate Supreme Control.
He commanded the banging of pots, driving sparrows to the sky,
never allowed to light, they flew until dying midair.

Mao wished to illustrate Supreme Control,
said sparrows ate too much grain,
he forced them to fly until they died midair
or had them caught in nets and poisoned.

Sparrows consume too much grain, he said,
and an estimated billion were killed.
Sparrows were caught in nets and poisoned;
dead birds of the Great Leap Forward.

An estimated billion were killed
and crop production increased:
dead birds of The Great Leap Forward
whose demise brought the invasions of insects.

Crop production increased for a time,
more rice for everyone,
but the invasion of insects
decimated every crop in sight.

There was more rice for everyone—
Mao's Supreme Control seemed confirmed.
Insects decimated every crop in sight
causing thirty-five million to starve.

Mao's Supreme Control seemed confirmed:
to stop hordes of insects, all crops were mowed.
Thirty-five million people starved,
All the sparrows, gone.

Crops were mowed, insects redirected.
Mao rethought the role sparrows
who feed insects to their chicks.
Decided it is better to conserve.

Mao rethought the role of sparrows,
an introduced species regarded as invasive,
who feed insects to their chicks.
Data linking sparrows to bluebird decline
remains sparse.

Spoleto Aubade

Predawn. Wood shutters open
to dew point and night's remnant shroud

of obscurity. Gary sleeps, but I cannot
for the thought of Italy, or maybe

it is vestiges of Sagrantino that wake
me before the sun's design. The field

beneath our villa is planted in fava.
Tall, it acquiesces to the breeze

that carries residual dreams
over the mountains to Assisi.

When harvested, the combine's growl
will strum Kansas to mind: my stomach

will swirl with homesickness and relief;
tart bouquet of the prodigal. Mockingbirds

and roses, ubiquitous prayers. Days
transpire into memory no matter

how quickly I write.

Just

Just now a subtle breeze, a trick of water, a dog's bark
        and another,
        and another.

Just now people with rifles,
        masked reporters,
        a camera.

Just now four rose bushes, a dozen blooms,
        three spent daisies,
        fox fern, blue pot,
        iris.

Just now a rampant virus, a floating ward, a parade of pundits, a jury.

Just now another pie, another pet, another letter
        in the mailbox.

Just now a president.

Just now a row of peas, a mound of squash, a trellis
        of tomatoes, pepper.

Just now satire and improv. The news; a president.

Just now the dishes, a flash, the laundry, bills, tall grass,
        a stimulus check.

Just now a woman asleep at night
        in her own bed
        inside her own home.

Just now the shadow of a cooper's hawk across the yard.
        No squirrels,
        no rabbits. Just now,
this president.

Just now protestors against a chain link fence
        around the White House
        Just   now,
        Black Lives Matter

Just now this book, a movie, a playlist, a distant conversation, run.
          Hulu, Netflix, Sling.

Just now, a president.

Just delivered: groceries, supplements, toiletries, pamphlets, pet food, clothes, medicine, books,
          a speech,
          leaflets
          lies.

Just now a noose, a shot, a decision, a red line, a machine,
          a cigarette, a toy
          a knee to the neck
          a storefront.

Just now a hot day, a polar vortex, a verdict, a tropical storm,
          hurricane season, tornado, bullets.

Just now, the arctic circle
          is one-hundred degrees today.
          Sea levels. Just now
a subtle breeze,

a trick of water, a dog's bark
          and another
          and another.

ODE TO QUICK TRIP

       I.

Who
      knows why—
excitement   boredom

the flashing pen light
from the ceiling smoke detector
piercing the darkness,
      eyelids.

A small town
      too—
no walking downstairs
      to a bustling body of people.
      No late-night cafés
or open bars,

      last call—
hours ago. All-night
grocery stores a casualty
of the pandemic
      they say

but there's a convenience
      store
3-minutes near

a Quick Trip
      to be exact—
always clean, well-lit
with an abundance of processed
      manna.

        II.

The store
        seems dim
in contrast to the bright canopy
        where vehicles, gas pumps
stand witness to the night. The pavement
shimmers, the air drips.
        Vestiges of a recent
        storm common
to hurricane season

        III.

Bratwursts,
        taquitos turn
on stainless steel rollers
beneath heat lamps. The donut case
is stocked
        like never before.

Personal-sized frozen pizzas
and hamburgers wrapped in cellophane
        wait near the microwave
as deli sandwiches
        and processed lunchmeat & cheese
packaged with Ritz crackers
        watch from the shelf
above an open cooler.

The clerk
        bubbles with 2 AM smiles
that would be annoying at 7 in the morning
        but is welcome,
is welcome right now above
this cache of late-midnight snacks,
        a lullaby of carbs to soothe
excitement, boredom.

III

YOU FIND YOURSELF IN KANSAS CITY

among house-proud women
and men who are mean with money.

You rent an apartment, the first
900 sq. ft. you've ever had all to yourself.

You don't mind that it is across the street from your mother's
where she can keep you both close and at arm's length

simultaneously because the space is cute—
because there is a porch for your plants—

until you find the HVAC for #8
is unpredictable, or rather it just doesn't work

even though the maintenance man bangs
on it with the kind of wrench plumbers use

in a show meant to convince you he's making repairs
and all three rooms stretching from west to east

and the tiny bathroom, too, remain forever
inclement. Below, a neighbor whose dog

barks, whose stereo blares, who is surly. Soon
you will discover the mice and will buy

crappy wood and wire traps at the hardware store
which you will toss away with pinched bodies

into the trash receptacle nearly every day
despite the fact that the cat in #10 visits

frequently to hunt, bringing them to you before the sun rises
to play with atop the bedcovers, a strange

kind of breakfast in bed.

VISITATION

Your son came by last Wednesday,
asking for more money.
He's off his meds again.
Left the hospital Sunday.

Your son was asking for money,
could use a pair of shoes.
He left the hospital on Sunday,
his bare feet were blue.

Your son could use a pair of shoes,
plans to stay at the Mission.
His bare toes were blue,
he's staving off delusions.

He plans to sleep at the Mission
or find his way to the north-town bridge.
He's staving off delusions,
hopes to find a warm bed.

He'll find his way to the north-town bridge,
and has never minded the streets.
He hopes to find a warm bed
since the forecast calls for sleet.

He has never minded the streets
or being off his meds.
Tonight's forecast calls for sleet.
I saw your son last Wednesday.

YIELD

Stonehenge is maintained with a push mower—
the groundskeeper marching back and forth
in crosshatch strips cutting the grass short, even
like a haircut, like a golf course. This is not

the way it looks once my husband passes the Philips Norelco
through hair left on my mother's pale scalp, a good ½ inch
the stylist *just could not bring herself* to shave.

Fluffs of charcoal dust the deck while silent
birds watch. The walnut tree sheds, too, dropping leaves
in early June. For ten years we assumed it a harbinger

of the tree's demise, but time has proven it does this
every season.

So Much Depends on a Brown Wicker Basket

After Matthew Olzman

Don't put all your eggs in one basket,
they said, which is odd because where
else would they go? No rooster

in the coop means eggs
would accumulate like cairns
crowding hens
from their purpose. Despite

Chicken-Little warnings, I place
eggs in a loose-weaved basket
shaped like a bassinet

where infant children sleep
until their cribs are less vacuous
and distant to their mothers.

One brown basket large
enough for a loaf of bread
or a few days' worth of eggs

snuggled together, bloom intact.
I have few other desires:
civil discourse in politics,

to walk my neighborhood
un-propositioned; slow
rain for the garden.

The basket sits beside the white
toaster on the kitchen counter
holding its gold. Watch

how it empties, refills in complete
odds with common sense,
our expectations of calamity.

Finding Mom

I have her ashes, her home,
all of her cluttered possessions
but am lost regarding her current
location.

The answer is in metaphysics, I'm told,
and write this in my journal.
I get as far as writing the question
in cursive, which I carry with me all day

because the problem with absolute
answers is that you begin think they exist
for everything.
        Metaphysically,
my root chakra
is lacking, so I do root chakra

things: eat root vegetables
and orange-colored fruit,
water the garden in bare
feet. The cardinal that visits
pecks sunflower seeds

from exhausted
heads that bob on the breeze.
The cardinal is a sign
that someone we love is near
and yes, this is where
my mother is—in the garden
and in the bird; in blooms
and in the grass. And she is in me

just as I am in the garden and
consequently, too, this
is where god might reside
if such a belief could
situate itself in my mind.

BACKYARD CHICKENS

A digital caution
from a friend:
the KKK marches
full regalia, broad daylight,
Richmond.

An old bad
dream returns to light.

All kinds of laws
never hold:
horse theft is still punishable
by hanging, men and women's
underthings never to be hung
on the same clothesline
on the same day.

In the backyard under the shade
of sweetgum
we build a chicken run
        for the coop
and though the day is hotter,

more humid
than any Floridian
could stand, we
measure and saw planks,
hammer nails until a frame
is formed to keep
        wire taut. Inside,
the kitchen is cool,
        anodyne
        is turkey sandwiches,
iced tea with lemon
        and a little sugar from the bowl.

Four newly hatched chicks
chirp for our nurture
from a box in the laundry room
          as we carve a life
away from the crisp
image of white sheets
on horseback.

Though the AC runs continuously,
          we leave open
window blinds, the front storm door,
          as shadows lean in contrast
to a heavy bronze sun
          moving slow as change,
          hot as a riot.

Prepared in Mind

Blind-slats slice sun across the floor of a former sitting room in an eighteenth-century house on campus; defunct fireplace in the corner, all tiles and old paint. Above student chatter of finals and graduation rise the *clop, clop* of horse-drawn carriages driven by tour guides in Confederate uniforms and a ship's bellow in the distance, not unlike a train's whistle piercing expansive plains, but distinct to coastlands. Passengers with hats and sunscreen, fanny packs and tennis shoes trickle sluggish into the open market for Sweetgrass baskets and Anson Mill Stone Ground Grits, then stroll King in search of Nordstrom's or Vineyard Vines, cash and cards burgeoning, thumbs hovered over touch screens surveying plaques on historic homes, casually researching signers of the declaration on cell phones, lift binoculars toward the walls of Sumter, dolphins breaching the harbor, Calhoun's bronze shadow cast across the square.

CATCH AND RELEASE

I hang clothes to dry on the drying rack set up on the small patio
of our condo that sits on the edge of the wooded wetlands
west of the Ashley. I am submerged in a chorus of tree frogs
and birdcall like I've never heard in all the years living
west of the Mississippi where sounds are distinct
and individual, embedded with stillness,
like the lilt of the Goldfinch. Home remains
the echo of a bullfrog's baritone off a farm pond,
the overhead whistle of a bald eagle, the peal
of Red-tailed hawk. The Lowcountry is flat as any desert,
only brackish with tidal waters and so dense in vegetation,
even the sky is green. Bird-voiced tree frogs blend their hymn
with the psalms of Carolina Wrens as the buzz
of cicadas underscore alligator barrage amid reeds.
Clinging to the vinyl siding, Five-lined, Broad Head
skinks mingle with Green Tree frogs, of the family Hylidae.
They feast, with sticky tongues, upon gnats and mosquitos
busy at the porch light at night. In the day, they come to explore
between the folds of damp jeans and t-shirts hanging
on the drying rack, become stowaways into the house
where I find them scaling shower doors or clinging
to the side of a toilet bowl, ready to leap.

I only believe in God on good days

after the cobwebs are cleared,
the sage smudged, after
the bed is made,
the paycheck cleared.

There is no god on any other day.
Only darkness at the threshold
of a narrow entry called *level*.

I cultivate acid hate, cast
stones like wishes at my shadow,
burn effigies of locust-branches
and muslin, the hair of a foe

collected under a full moon—
the witching moon, a wreath
of thorns, thick

around the crown.
I want vengeance—
            a satisfying list of enemies
each name struck through
like life, bones kindling
this all-consuming flame.

Matthew Prompts Evacuation

Our first evacuation, we fled to Kansas City,
and our house was crushed by a hickory tree.
We stayed six-weeks in a Charleston hotel suite
leaving our cat at a friend's house.

Our house was crushed by a hickory tree,
and we moved to an apartment near downtown,
brought our cat from the friend's house,
who hissed at the dog three doors down.

We'd found an apartment close to downtown
making our commute to work a dream.
A mean dog lived three doors down,
but family would be visiting for the holidays.

Our commute to the college was a dream
though the apartment had no charm.
Family would visit for the holidays,
and the house would get a remodel.

Though the apartment had no charm
and we fought daily with adjusters,
we were glad for the house remodel
as fall semester stretched into spring.

While we fought daily with insurance adjusters,
a full-time position opened up at the college.
The fall semester stretched into spring
when I submitted my CV and transcripts

for the full-time position at the college.
An adjunct for many years, and wanting stability,
I submitted my application, CV and transcripts,
then was invited for a Skype interview.

An adjunct for many years, and wanting stability,
even though life was in chaos,
I prepared carefully for the Skype interview;
I was certain my candidacy was strong enough.

Even though life was in chaos
and we were in the middle of a remodel.
I was certain my candidacy was strong enough,
but the Chair said I hadn't made the cut.

I threw myself into the house remodel
thinking of our thirty-year mortgage.
the Chair said I hadn't made the cut.
and I went back to teaching as an adjunct.

Thinking of our thirty-year mortgage
and watching dumpsters fill with ruined furniture,
I went back to teaching as an adjunct
and negotiating with insurance adjusters.

Watching dumpsters fill with ruined furniture
and winter clouds morphing into spring rain,
I negotiated with insurance adjusters
to prove we needed every penny.

Winter clouds morphed into spring rain
as large trucks tore up the yard,
I proved we needed every penny,
and noticed a rose blooming in the yard.

Large trucks tore up the front yard
but I couldn't worry about landscaping.
Of the rose blooming in the yard,
I took a picture for posterity.

I couldn't worry about landscaping
or the wrens nesting in the trash bin;
I took pictures for posterity
the day of final inspection.

Wrens nested in the garbage bin
as we moved our books out of storage.
After the adjuster's final inspection,
we'd been out of house seven months.

Flag and Signal

Midmorning. A gray squirrel scolds Olive
from a leafless limb of the sweet gum tree.

Its complaints against her are ceaseless,
grow more adamant as do mine against the neighbors

who are not bad per se, only young and wealthy.
It was quieter when the house next door

was in probate: roof collapsed, yard a sylvan haven
for possums, raccoons, owls, foxes, strays

right here in the middle of the city. Olive stalks
a scuttling sound beneath the pine mulch

under the Spirea screen I've planted between
our porch and the street where I hide from dog walkers

and joggers who've grown in number
since the new house was built a couple lots down.

A dozen more houses have been remodeled, flipped
since then, the scent of treated-lumber

wafting gentrification through the neighborhood
distracting us from the ocean's acidic rising.

Vespers

I caught the evening breeze
instead of the evening news
and am much better for the choice.

There are no arguments
to be had with the wind,
only surrender to what is

which will never change
to suit me or an agenda.
Thankfulness and grace, like birds,

go unnoticed. They are too
common, have no website.
In the garden, they fail to worry

over how green the grass,
where to find more. There is
only this seed, this feather,
this breeze.

QUARTERLY SCREENING

In the waiting room at the Head and Neck Tumor Clinic,
I read used pulp fiction, something published in the 70s.

A large suction cup blaps the window above my head
startling me, then disappears. The window washer crawls out of sight.

A couple arrives, sits across from me. The man is talkative,
the woman hasn't the privilege. She wears a tracheal cap around her throat.

I smile, take the woman to be the man's wife. She never
makes eye contact, only writes notes to the man

on a small dry erase board she's pulled from her bag.
The man assumes I am not the patient, that I wait

for someone else. I know to count myself lucky
in his mistake, which is why

I always bring something to read or knit.
It sometimes takes three hours to see the specialist

whose clinic is on Mondays. I am relieved when called
back to exam room four with a window

looking out over downtown, its water and its bridges.

OWLS AT MIDDAY

Keeping the garden wet, the bird baths full,
these are the primary tasks in Charleston's
drought, not so dry as the high desert

in any given moment, nor Northeast Kansas
during the 80s. This landscape is
of porous, sandy soil, tall thirsty trees,

of marshes (and marshes). Creeks run
wider, deeper than the Rio Grande,
the Kansas River.

Tired is the grass that burns in the sun,
bedding plants lay dwarfed and unbloomed
in their beds as robins dance in the sprinkler's

overshot droplets. A midday omen
or sign of luck, two barred owls visit
the birdbath's shallow basin.

Wings dot sudden with stars,
their eyes, tunnels into the other-world,
echo my mother's feathered call.

REFRAIN

We follow the sun west,
          arrive in Globe dense with luggage—
unfold our map into a momentary family.
Our coordinates:
          mother, father,
          grandparents,
          a child
newly arrived from the world overlooked
except when people loved are born
or die, bringing together strange relations
for hello and goodbye.

In this week before Christmas, I hope to brush
against the delicate early days of new motherhood
brief as a hiccup, a gas bubble, nurture this child
with love still bright in his eyes

while the family sleeps silent through the night,
while the sun pulses somewhere above unfamiliar
hemispheres, blinding stars shining nonetheless,
while the moon collects night into itself and coyotes carol
beyond azure ridges of saguaro cacti.

His breath, fragrant with breast milk; his cries a kitten's mew
from new lungs. He turns toward light, towards his mother's face.
Within moments we'll pack our bags again, fly opposite
the new year, our bones hollow as an O'Keefe still life,
hopes as bland as a month-old fir waiting on the curb.

Notes

"Ad Astra Per Aspera" means, "To the stars through difficulties" and is the Kansas state motto.

"The Umbrella Man" is a British song written by James Cavanaugh, Larry Stock and Vincent Rose. Dizzie Gellespie recorded his version in July 1952.

"Prepared in Mind" comes from the South Carolina state motto, "Animis Opibusque Parati"

"She Flies With Her Own Wings" is the Oregon state motto.

ACKNOWLEDGEMENTS

Many thanks to the following journals and anthologies in which these poems first appeared, sometimes in different versions: *Chiron Review*, "Washington Street"; *Limp Wrist*, "After the Ban"; *Pensive*, "Finding Mom"; *Mom Egg Review VOX*, "Her Own Girl"; *Kakalak*, "One Saturday in March, We Deal Again with Mortality"; *Tipton Poetry Review*, "Preservation" (featured poem) and "Planting Season"; *The Strategic Poet*, "Land of the Southwind"; *Ice on a Hot Stove*, "Just Now" and "Yield"; *Cimarron Review*, "Yield"; *Fall Lines*, "Dead Birds of the Great Leap Forward"; *Emrys Review*, "Just"; *Witty Partition*, "Maple"; *Kakalak*, "The Owls at Midday"; and *Willawaw Journal*, "You Find Yourself in Kansas City."

I am deeply indebted to the Vermont Studio Center and the Kimmel Harding-Nelson Center for the Arts for providing me time, support, and room to write. Many of the poems in this collection were dreamt of or drafted during residencies at these art centers.

Thank you to Alison Mero and Clemson University Press for supporting the publication of poetry through their partnership with Converse University Low Residency MFA program and the Clemson-Converse Literature series.

My heartfelt gratitude for the continued guidance and camaraderie of Converse University mentors, Rick Mulkey, Denise Duhamel, Suzanne Cleary, Richard Tillinghast, Marlin Barton, Bob Olmsted, and Leslie Pietrzyk. My well-being and that of this book would be lost without them.

To friends Jonathan Bohr Heinen and Esther Lee, who inspire and encourage me in countless ways and in every endeavor.

Undying gratitude and love to my aunt, Nancie Thomas, for believing in me even before I believed in myself; my father, John Lotz, who is as excited about this collection as I; my daughter, Casey Bruner, who believes in me still, and my mother, Patricia Thomas, whose voice continues to guide my life, my passion, and my art.

And most importantly, fathomless love and appreciation to Gary Jackson, sun to my solar system, moon to my tide.